W9-CNE-904

NATURAL DISASTERS

VOLCANOES

ABDO
Publishing Company

Rochelle Baltzer

Big Buddy BOOKS
Natural Disasters

VISIT US AT
www.abdopublishing.com

Published by ABDO Publishing Company, 8000 West 78th Street, Edina, Minnesota 55439.

Printed in the United States of America, North Mankato, Minnesota.
052011
092011

 PRINTED ON RECYCLED PAPER

Coordinating Series Editor: Sarah Tieck
Contributing Editors: Megan M. Gunderson, BreAnn Rumsch, Marcia Zappa
Graphic Design: Adam Craven
Cover Photograph: *Shutterstock*: beboy.
Interior Photographs/Illustrations: *AP Photo*: Courtesy USDA Forest Service, Mount St. Helens National Volcanic Monument, file. (p. 27); *Getty Images*: David Hogan (p. 23), Ulet Ifansasti (p. 23), G. Brad Lewis (p. 19), Eric Meola (p. 5), Carsten Peter (p. 19); *iStockphoto*: ©iStockphoto.com/guenterguni (p. 7); *NASA*: NASA Planetary Photo Journal Collection (p. 30); *Photo Researchers, Inc.*: BSIP (p. 9), Gary Hincks (p. 11) Images & Volcanoes (p. 15), Stephen & Donna O'Meara (p. 29); *Photolibrary*: Doug Cheeseman (p. 13), Olivier Grunewald (p. 21), James Mason (pp. 25, 27); *Shutterstock*: bierchen (p. 7), Sherri R. Camp (p. 17), Andrew Kua Seng How (p. 15), Rigucci (p. 25), robootb (p. 25).

Library of Congress Cataloging-in-Publication Data

Baltzer, Rochelle, 1982-
 Volcanoes / Rochelle Baltzer.
   p. cm. -- (Natural disasters)
 ISBN 978-1-61783-035-8
 1. Volcanoes--Juvenile literature. I. Title.
 QE521.3.B335 2012
 551.21--dc22
                                    2011013147

VOLCANOES

CONTENTS

POWERFUL VOLCANOES

A towering mountain begins to rumble. Then all of a sudden, *boom*! The ground shakes. Steam and rocks burst from the mountain. Lava flows down its side. A volcano is **erupting**!

When a volcano erupts, it is a natural disaster. Natural disasters happen because of weather or changes inside Earth. They can badly harm areas. They even take lives. By learning about them, people are better able to stay safe.

The word *volcano* comes from Vulcan, the Roman god of fire.

RUMBLE AND TUMBLE

A volcano is a deep opening, or vent, in Earth's surface. It lets out **magma**, gas, and rock. When magma **erupts** onto Earth's surface, it is called lava.

Lava hardens into rock as it cools. After many eruptions, rock builds up around a vent. Over time, it forms a volcanic mountain. This is also called a volcano.

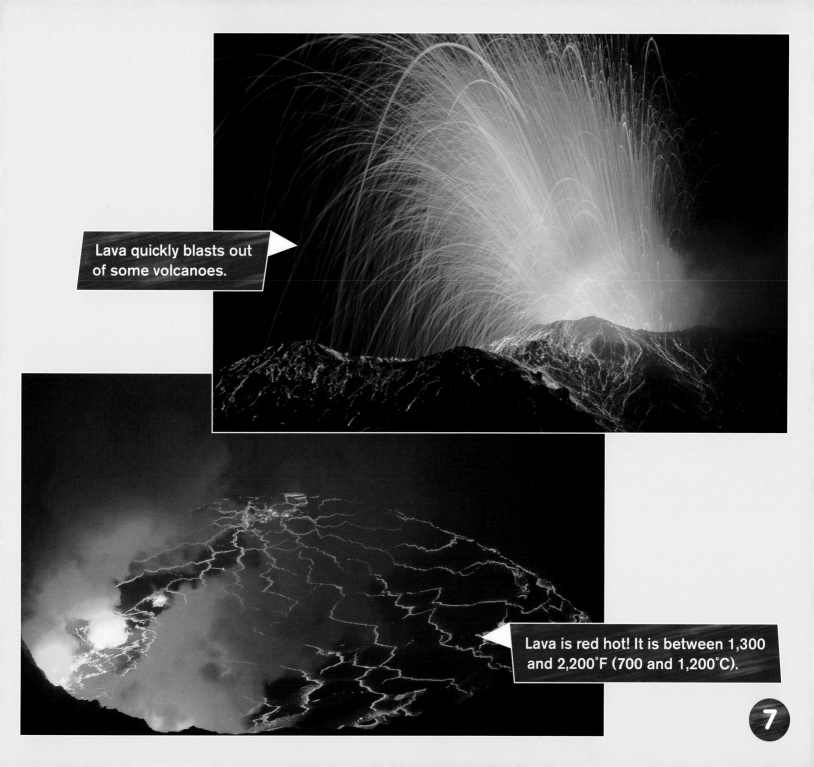

Lava quickly blasts out of some volcanoes.

Lava is red hot! It is between 1,300 and 2,200°F (700 and 1,200°C).

7

UNDER PRESSURE

Deep inside Earth, **magma** is less **dense** than surrounding rock. This causes it to rise. It collects in a hollow area called a magma chamber. As magma fills the chamber, **pressure** builds. Finally, it is pushed out through the vent.

BREAKING NEWS

Magma often has gas in it. The more gas it has, the more powerful the blast usually is. Often, rocks and ash shoot into the air with lava.

INSIDE A VOLCANO

main vent

vent

magma chamber

9

RING OF FIRE

Earth is made up of four **layers**. The **crust** is the outermost layer. It is split into huge plates. They fit together like pieces of a jigsaw puzzle. The plates slowly move on a layer of **magma**.

Magma leaks out between the plates. This is where most volcanoes form. Many are along the Ring of Fire. The Ring of Fire lines up with a plate under the Pacific Ocean.

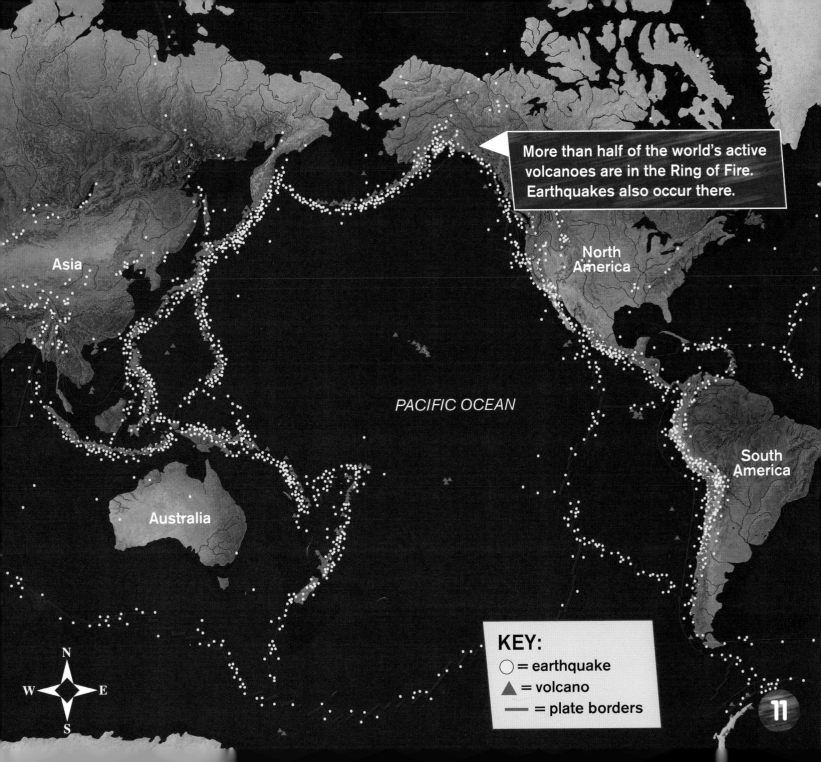

More than half of the world's active volcanoes are in the Ring of Fire. Earthquakes also occur there.

Asia

North America

PACIFIC OCEAN

Australia

South America

N
W E
S

KEY:
○ = earthquake
▲ = volcano
▬ = plate borders

11

TYPES OF VOLCANOES

There are several types of volcanoes. The most common are shield volcanoes, composite volcanoes, and **cinder** cones.

Inside a shield volcano, **magma** is thin. It spreads out easily during an **eruption**. Over time, this forms a low, wide volcano. Shield volcanoes are some of the largest.

Hawaii's Mauna Loa is a shield volcano.

BREAKING NEWS

Volcanoes are underwater, too. Over time, they can build up to form islands. That's how Hawaii formed!

13

A composite volcano is usually smaller than a shield volcano. Sometimes, it **erupts** lava. Other times, ash, **cinders**, and rock blast out. They pile up in **layers**. This forms a tall, steep volcano.

A cinder cone is a cone-shaped volcano. Cinders, ash, and sometimes lava erupt from it. The loose cinders and ash may build up to form a steep hill.

Mount Fuji is a composite volcano in Japan.

Parícutin is a cinder cone in Mexico.

CHANGING EARTH

When volcanoes **erupt**, they change Earth's surface. Over time, rock, ash, and lava can fill in valleys and bury hills.

After a powerful blast, the top of a volcano can cave in. This leaves a crater or caldera. A crater is a bowl-shaped area. A caldera is like a crater, only bigger.

Thousands of years ago, an eruption left a caldera. The caldera filled with water over time. Today, it is known as Crater Lake in Oregon.

17

STUDYING VOLCANOES

Scientists study volcanoes to **predict** when they will **erupt**. Then, they can warn people. They measure changes in the volcano's shape. Sometimes, gases may come out of its vents. Or, small **earthquakes** happen nearby. These are warning signs.

After an eruption, scientists rate its power. They track how high it went and the amount of lava let out. This helps them better understand these events.

Scientists collect magma to study.

Sometimes, scientists go in a volcano. They may wear special suits to stay safe.

19

DISASTER ZONE

Some volcanoes cause much harm when they **erupt**. Ash and lava can destroy towns and natural areas. Ash and gas can bury, burn, or poison people and animals.

After an eruption, communities come together. People who are trapped or hurt are brought to safe places. Workers clean up ash-covered areas. They help rebuild towns.

Ash and lava can bury homes.

VOLCANO SAFETY

Most scientists call a volcano active if it has **erupted** in the past 10,000 years. Safety plans are important in areas near active volcanoes. Officials give warnings if a volcano is likely to erupt. Then, people leave the area.

VOLCANO
EVACUATION ROUTE

BREAKING NEWS

People who live near an active volcano keep safety kits in their homes. A kit has masks, goggles, first-aid items, a radio, a flashlight, food, and water.

Marked paths and roads are the safest, fastest ways to reach safety.

When many people leave at once, it may take extra time to reach safety.

CASE STUDY:
MOUNT SAINT HELENS

Mount Saint Helens in Washington hadn't **erupted** in more than 100 years. But in March 1980, it began to rumble. Steam started to come out of its top.

On May 18, an **earthquake** struck. It caused a major **landslide**. This opened up a crack on the volcano. Then, it erupted! Hot gas, ash, and rock shot out. Ash blew across eastern Washington and ten other states!

Scientists say ash, gas, and rock shot out as fast as 300 miles (480 km) per hour!

Mount Saint Helens is a composite volcano.

Canada
United States
WASHINGTON
▲ Mount Saint Helens
Pacific Ocean
OREGON
IDAHO

The **eruption** lasted nine hours. Hot ash led to fires. The heat melted snow on the volcano. This caused floods and more **landslides**. Forests, farms, roads, and trails were destroyed.

This event was one of North America's most powerful eruptions. Officials had warned people to leave the area. Still, 57 people were killed and many more were hurt. Scientists still study Mount Saint Helens. They think it could erupt again someday.

The blast took more than 1,000 feet (300 m) off the top of Mount Saint Helens. It left a huge crater.

The Mount Saint Helens blast changed the land around it. Forests (*above*) were destroyed by lava, which hardened into rock (*left*).

FORCE
OF NATURE

Volcanic **eruptions** change Earth's surface and cause much harm. Yet, their rock and ash can be useful. Rock is used to build roads, and ash forms good farming soil.

Scientists continue to study volcanoes. They learn new ways to keep people safe. This can save lives!

Lava and rocks can burn and knock down forests.

NEWS FLASH!

- A volcano on the Italian island of Stromboli is very active. It has been **erupting** on and off for more than 2,000 years!

- In AD 79, Italy's Mount Vesuvius erupted. Rocks and ash buried the city of Pompeii. The city was found again in the 1700s. Since then, people have been learning about its history.

- Indonesia has more than 100 active volcanoes. That is more than any other country.

- There are volcanoes on other planets. Olympus Mons is on Mars. It is our solar system's largest volcano.

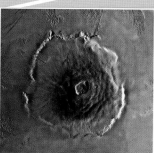

IMPORTANT WORDS

cinder a piece of lava from an erupting volcano.

crust the hard outer covering of a planet.

dense heavy compared to other objects of the same size.

earthquake (UHRTH-kwayk) a shaking of a part of the earth.

erupt to burst out suddenly. When this happens, it is called an eruption.

landslide a mass of soil or rock that slides down a slope.

layer a part that is on top of or underneath another part.

magma melted rock beneath Earth's surface.

predict to say something is going to happen before it does.

pressure (PREH-shuhr) the pushing of a force against an opposing force.

WEB SITES

To learn more about volcanoes, visit ABDO Publishing Company online. Web sites about volcanoes are featured on our Book Links page. These links are routinely monitored and updated to provide the most current information available.

www.abdopublishing.com

INDEX